GYMNASTICS

RULES, EQUIPMENT AND KEY ROUTINE TIPS

by Tracy Nelson Maurer

raintree

a Capstone company — publishers for children

Raintree is an imprint of Capstone Global Library Limited, a company incorporated in England and Wales having its registered office at 264 Banbury Road, Oxford, OX2 7DY – Registered company number: 6695582

www.raintree.co.uk
myorders@raintree.co.uk

Edited by Bradley Cole
Designed by Sarah Bennett and Katy LaVigne
Picture research by Eric Gohl
Production by Kathy McColley
Originated by Capstone Global Library Limited

ISBN 978-1-4747-4281-8
21 20 19 18 17
10 9 8 7 6 5 4 3 2 1

ISBN 978-1-4747-4283-2
22 21 20 19 18
10 9 8 7 6 5 4 3 2 1

British Library Cataloguing in Publication Data
A full catalogue record for this book is available from the British Library.

Acknowledgements
We would like to thank the following for permission to reproduce photographs: Alamy Stock Photo: Aflo Co., Ltd., 17; Dreamstime: Saltcityphotography, cover; iStockphoto: Tassii, 15; Newscom: EFE/Javier Etxezarreta, 6 (right); Shutterstock: 4Max, 1 (background, top right), Air Images, 4, ITALO, 1, 11 (left), Leonard Zhukovsky, 5, 19, 21, Lilyana Vynogradova, 6 (left), 11 (right), Luigi Fardella, 13, Mitrofanov Alexander, 7 (right), roibu, cover (background), 1 (background, top left & middle), Sasha Samardzija, 9, testing, 7 (left)
Design Elements:
Shutterstock

We would like to thank Paige Roth for her invaluable help in the preparation of this book.

Printed and bound in India

CONTENTS

Gymnastics fun

Running! Jumping! Flipping! Gymnastics is full of action. Girls and boys around the world join gymnastics clubs. They build strength and learn about flexibility and balance. Many have dreams of winning an Olympic gold medal one day. Do you dream of being a gymnast?

"I kind of do think of myself as a superhero and just flying high, and doing these crazy flips."

– *Gabby Douglas,*
US Olympic gold medalist

5

Types of gymnastics

ARTISTIC GYMNASTICS

Artistic gymnastics has been part of the Olympics since the first competition in 1896. Women's events include the vault, uneven bars, balance beam and floor exercise. Men's events are the vault, floor exercise, pommel horse, still rings, parallel bars and horizontal bar.

TRAMPOLINE AND TUMBLING

All gymnasts learn basic tumbling moves, including the somersault. Some gymnasts advance to trampoline, power tumbling, **synchronized** trampoline and double mini-trampoline events. Trampolining became an Olympic sport in 2000.

RHYTHMIC GYMNASTICS

Rhythmic gymnasts perform routines to music. They compete in five events. Each event uses different props, including a rope, a hoop, a ball, clubs and ribbon. Rhythmic gymnastics was added to the Summer Olympics in 1984.

ACROBATIC GYMNASTICS

Shows such as Cirque du Soleil often feature high-energy **acrobatics**. Acrobatic gymnasts compete in groups or pairs. Events include pairs, mixed pairs, women's group and men's group.

synchronized when two or more people perform the same movements at the same time

acrobatics movements borrowed from gymnastics, such as handstands, flips and forward rolls

CHAPTER 1

Geared up

Gymnastic club gyms have mats, bars, rings and other equipment. Club gyms are safe places to learn and practise skills. Gymnasts use a specific piece of equipment or **apparatus** to perform certain skills. They do flips off a **vaulting horse**. They practise moves and exercises with the rings.

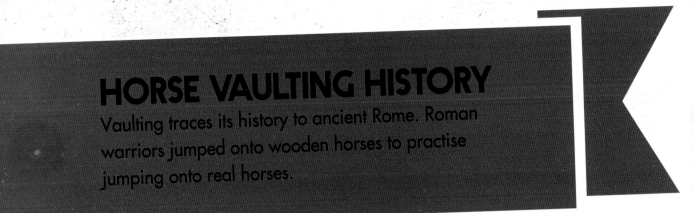

HORSE VAULTING HISTORY

Vaulting traces its history to ancient Rome. Roman warriors jumped onto wooden horses to practise jumping onto real horses.

apparatus equipment used in gymnastics, such as the balance beam or uneven bars

vaulting horse apparatus for launching a gymnast into the air to perform flips and twists

9

What to wear

Gymnasts wear snug clothing that won't catch on equipment. Girls wear one-piece **leotards** for competitions and practices. They may also wear shorts over the leotards at practices.

Boys wear shorts and T-shirts at practices. They compete in sleeveless leotards and **stirrups**. Teams usually compete in matching uniforms.

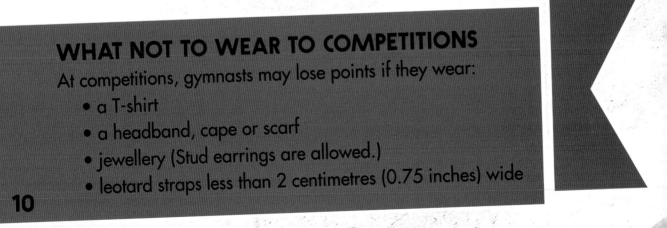

WHAT NOT TO WEAR TO COMPETITIONS

At competitions, gymnasts may lose points if they wear:
- a T-shirt
- a headband, cape or scarf
- jewellery (Stud earrings are allowed.)
- leotard straps less than 2 centimetres (0.75 inches) wide

leotard snug and stretchy one-piece uniform worn by female gymnasts and dancers

stirrups stretchy trousers with a band of elastic at the bottom of each leg to keep them in place

11

CHAPTER 2

Form and routines

Gymnasts try to keep their bodies in certain forms or shapes when they perform. Toes curve downwards. Ankles stay together most of the time.

The mat is for practising. Beginners learn rolls, tucks and cartwheels. After gymnasts learn basic skills, they try more difficult tricks. They perform a series of tricks called a **routine** at competitions. Good form and a bit of flair leads to higher scores.

HOW LONG?

Some routines last more than 1 minute. The floor routine is up to 90 seconds of non-stop action. Other events, such as the vault, take just 6 or 7 seconds. All routines need hours of practice.

routine series of tricks linked one after another in a performance on one apparatus

Practice

Gymnasts train with coaches at gyms to learn new skills. They do push-ups, sit-ups and other exercises to build upper body and core strength. Exercises such as star jumps or jumping with a skipping rope increase **stamina**.

FUEL YOUR BODY!

Gymnasts need good fuel! They eat balanced meals with plenty of lean proteins, whole grains and dairy foods. Healthy snacks include yogurt and porridge.

stamina energy and strength to keep doing something for a long time

CHAPTER 3

Rules of the sport

Judges look for smooth and strong movements. Jumps and vaults with great height and distance earn good scores. Judges expect landings without wobbles too.

The Junior Olympics scoring starts gymnasts with a score of 10.0. Points are subtracted for mistakes such as missing requirements and other errors.

TRICK NAMES

New tricks are often named after the first gymnast to perform it at a worldwide competition. Kurt Thomas is known for the Thomas Flair. It is a spinning move done with the legs held in a V shape. He first performed this move in 1977 in Barcelona, Spain.

"When I began my career, I just wanted to do cartwheels."

– *Romanian Olympian Nadia Comaneci, in* Letters to a Young Gymnast

NADIA COMANECI

FACT

Romanian Nadia Comaneci achieved the first perfect score in women's gymnastics at the Olympics in 1976 in Montreal, Canada.

If you dream of competing in the Olympics, you should join a gym that trains **elite** gymnasts. Only elite gymnasts may compete at the national and international level. With practice, skill and determination, your dreams can come true!

2016 OLYMPICS

FACT
Gymnasts must turn 16 years of age during the calendar year to compete in the Olympics.

elite describes gymnasts who are among the best

ELITE COMPETITION SCORING

Difficulty Score (D) + Execution Score (E) = Final Score (F)
D scores start at 0 and increase with points for performing each difficult skill.
E scores start at 10 and decrease with errors.

CHAPTER 4

Performance tips

Great gymnasts, such as Simone Biles, make their routines look easy. They shine with confidence. But they have fallen countless times along the way. What's their secret to success? They learn from the falls and work even harder.

TIPS AND TRICKS

- Slippery hands? Try chalk powder on your hands – and maybe even your feet!

- When you fall, tuck and roll in the direction you're already moving. Cross your arms over your chest to prevent injuries to your fingers, wrists or elbows.

- Practise your landings. Bend your knees when you hit the mat. Hold your arms out straight with your palms down for extra balance.

- Strike a final pose with straight legs, arched back, chin up and arms high. Smile with gold-medal confidence!

"Before I begin a routine I just think 'confidence' and how many times I've done this routine."

– *US Olympic gymnast Simone Biles*

Glossary

acrobatics movements borrowed from gymnastics, such as handstands, flips and forward rolls

apparatus equipment used in gymnastics, such as the balance beam or uneven bars

elite describes gymnasts who are among the best

leotard snug and stretchy one-piece uniform worn by female gymnasts and dancers

routine series of tricks linked one after another in a performance on one apparatus

stamina energy and strength to keep doing something for a long time

stirrups stretchy trousers with a band of elastic at the bottom of each leg to keep them in place

synchronized when two or more people perform the same movements at the same time

vaulting horse apparatus for launching a gymnast into the air to perform flips and twists

Read more

Great Olympic Moments (The Olympics), Michael Hurley (Raintree, 2012)

Gymnastics (Usborne Spectator Guides), Sam Lake (Usborne Publishing Ltd, 2016)

The World's Greatest Olympians (The Olympics), Michael Hurley (Raintree, 2012)

Websites

www.british-gymnastics.org
Learn about gymnastics from the official UK governing body.

www.british-gymnastics.org/gymnast-profiles
Discover more about the UK's professional gymnasts.

www.dkfindout.com/uk/sports/gymnastics/
Learn more about gymnastics!

Index